FINISHING LINE PRESS

www.finishinglinepress.com

THE SKY WEEPS WITH US

poems by

Laurel S. Peterson

Finishing Line Press
Georgetown, Kentucky

THE SKY WEEPS WITH US

For all the ones we've lost, and for all who remain—
and especially, and always, for Van

ACKNOWLEDGMENTS

The Champagne Journal: "Macy," "Gratitude," "Drought"
Connecticut Literary Anthology 2023: "In the Gouffre de Padirac"
The Same: "Fog"
Verse Virtual: "Liz," "Dad," "Aunt Arlene," "Places to Feel"

Publisher: Leah Huete de Maines
Editor: Christen Kincaid
Cover Art: Laurel S. Peterson
Author Photo: Ute-Christin Cowan, UC Photography
Cover Design: Elizabeth Maines McCleavy

Order online: www.finishinglinepress.com
also available on amazon.com

Author inquiries and mail orders:
Finishing Line Press
PO Box 1626
Georgetown, Kentucky 40324
USA

Contents

QUIET

The sky is half lit, shaded by clouds,
the traffic's morning grumble abated,
a holiday pause for dump trucks and postal vans.

The squirrels curl in their nests,
giving the birds full forage at the feeder.
Even the wind has calmed,
sifting only occasionally over a branch,
or tickling winter's dried flower stalks.

This living silence should
have been our last two COVID years,
a silence into which we could thaw
our aggrieved and lonely hearts,
but even after all this time, we still
see our own faces and flinch.

MOM

What has happened, my mother cried after Dad had his first TIA, *to my handsome Navy pilot?*, he who had fallen next to the coffee table he'd built himself, and then the ambulance came, we came, he couldn't comprehend time or numbers, the man who had measured those boards, fit them together, landed 747s in ice and thunder, and she turned to me, standing in the part of the basement kept locked against intruders and filled with jars of tomato sauce, dried beans, pickles, and cleaning supplies against the end of civilization—which had just arrived—and cried, *where has he gone?* and all I could do was hold her.

FOG

The fog lay so thick
we could barely see our way,
white line burrowing
into floating mist
that cleared and clouded like tide pools.
Age stretches out its pathetic
and horrifying tentacles,
and we are unsteady,
I am unsteady,
unsure of the line,
if it's there at all.

You've always been the breakwater—
Now your body claims its pains,
hard edges of barnacle and urchin spine
and the regular waves sustain and batter,
like this fog that shreds and closes
on whim, shape-shifting in and out
of childhood monsters.
There's always a gull,
flap-hopping greedy toward us,
hard to make out in the swirls
of white camouflage,
hard to escape.

LIZ

And that day when I found out I'd missed the funeral and no
one had told me when or where and I wondered if I hadn't
been a good enough friend to be invited, as if it were a party
or a contest, and of course ascribed it to grief or oversight
or the loss of a phone number, even though her husband
had called to let me know she was dying….and there I was
in a hotel in New York after my husband's bladder cancer
surgery and we were headed to Sel et Poivre and I texted her
a picture of the cavern of the street and said *I miss you* and
do you think Cuomo's really in the shit now and then, she was
gone.

AUNT ARLENE

I should have called
just one more time.
I knew you were close,
legs swollen and bleeding
at the faintest touch,
unable to walk,
but your laugh still loud.
You're a good kid—
that's what you said,
even in my fifties,
and I was grateful.

Now, you've disappeared,
just the latest in a line
of vanishings,
like puffs of smoke lingering
over a vacant railroad track,
an endless series
of little white clouds
hovering in empty air.

MORGAN

And you, walking the mall, racing me and telling me to
slow down when it was you pushing yourself, trying to keep
ahead of the cancer, walking yourself free, and on the way,
telling me the story of your caregiver with the head twitched
by spirits. *Spirits?* You said, *Who's to know?* You who in the
last weeks of your life turned to the Unitarian Church and
told me how angry you were. *Why me? No really. Why me?*
How could I tell you it's all of us and none of it's fair, when
you at forty-six, your beautiful self erased to but a twig, had
six weeks left. And then none.

HUSBAND

And the afternoon we were walking into the condo, a new joy
against pandemic darkness, a place to escape but your phone
tracked you down, and you stayed outside. So I wouldn't
learn the news that way? And when you came in, up the
stairs and across to the grey velvet chair where I sat, your face
blank and maybe angry, hurt your body would treat you this
way when you'd given it tennis and running and weights and
fish dinners, and you said, "It's cancer."

THEN CAME COVID

And we all scurried to our corners, huddling over the blue
light of our screens, shivering, trying to breathe less in public
places, buying food at six AM, and old mothers complained
of loneliness, and young mothers of total exhaustion, and the
Thai restaurant started delivering but the Venezuelan coffee
place disappeared, and we, with no children and remote
jobs, drank cocktails outside in thirty degree weather in our
parkas and boots overlooking the water while librarians
wiped down books, and one friend disinfected delivered
groceries, and another, one of thousands in nursing homes
or hospitals or driving UPS trucks, died.

DAD

And there you were in your recliner, the dinner tray served
while we packed to leave, Mom for the night and us to return
to Connecticut, and you bit into your grilled cheese, a long
string of it looping between your lips and the sandwich,
and your blank puzzled look at my *Oh Dad*, as if you could
comprehend neither the problem nor the solution, you who
had lifted a jet off a carrier over the Mediterranean, who had
built the table on which I write this, searching out antique
boards with just the right amount of knot, whose hands I still
see running carefully over marble sculpture or Persian rugs,
teaching me touch, and then, a week later, you were gone.

FILLING THE BIRDBATH

A hunk of concrete dropped off
the birdbath yesterday when
I readjusted the bowl again
I think the deer come to drink at dusk
their supple tongues
nudging the flat to an angle

and now I'm unsure if it's
steady enough to last
another winter
may crumble it
and a new one won't be this
pocked hand-me-down
ivy climbing its base
thirty years of soft feathers
fluttering in its mouth at twilight

FOG II

The fog kisses the beach this morning
but refuses landfall,
preferring instead to muffle
the water view,
the noise of the waves
who just bump the shore gently,
like a hip bump, wife to beloved husband
of many years, invitation, maybe.

Perhaps the fog is lonely,
unloved as it so often is,
hovering over its damp soul;
I cannot see into its swirling, cold heart,
nor into my own,
which is wounded and floating
just out of reach.

PAIN

Some nights bones ache
so deep it's below the level of feeling.
Fingers pressed into tendons or joints
release tenderness so extreme
it's all the body can do
to keep from screaming.
A shoulder's sorrow
rings down the arm and out
through the fingers,
a wave that washes it clean
or pretends to.

DROUGHT

Then came the summer without water, and Lake Mead
dropped so low the skeletons of old Mafia hits emerged
and Spanish Stonehenge rose from Peraleda de la Mata as
the Valdecañas reservoir shrank, and the garden soil grew
cracked, and we worried about hunger—because, well,
Ukraine—and we worried about heating oil—because, well,
Russia—and gas prices rose above five dollars a gallon and
people had to choose among chicken, antibiotics, rent, and
air-conditioning in one-hundred-degree heat, and rain
threatened and passed over even as we knelt on the parched
ground surrounded by an acre of only crabgrass and dirt now
under the empty sky with our drums and prayers, pleading.

THIS MORNING ON MY WALK

a howl from a side street, muted, as if from a shuttered
interior room. An older child, I imagine, wordless, perhaps
unable, except through that forlorn wail, to express distress,
hollow somewhere, like all of us, like an underground cavern
that winds deeper and deeper toward the earth's core, a core
that spits up fiery breath, something unquenchable, a river
that scorches our words to ash.

IN THE GOUFFRE DE PADIRAC

Half lit and slick, stone floors
guide us along the underground river
by rock pools,
                 water collected
over thousands of years, dripped
into stalactites and stalagmites.

You and I follow the paths around,
         up the stairs and down,
taking photos in the half-lit dark
while I try to remember
to breathe.
         There's enough air
down here, I tell myself,
even if the lights go out

and we have to feel our way
in a long, sparkling line
of cell phone flashlights
back up
                 the five hundred
        slippery steps
to sunlight.

But it's more than satiny
limewater on stone
        or the press
of darkness that leaves me
                 unstable
in this alternate world.

We are losing the path,
             you and I,
as the future forms stone around us.

AUNT ARLENE II

I didn't call you at the end, even though I should have,
but finally we only knew each other in the relative way,
where we could talk about your kids and grandkids—but I
didn't have kids—so we talked about the pirate games you
and Mom played as children, spying enemies out over the
cranberry bogs and burying treasure in the attic, treasure
I searched for all through childhood, and your trips to
Germany to see your son, and buying Waterford crystal in
Ireland—and in our last phone call you made me promise
to go to Hammonasset Beach near our Branford home
because, you said, *Enjoy every minute*, but I'm failing you. I
hear the minutes creak by as I sit in your back yard after the
memorial service, talking to your grandson's girlfriend about
medical equipment sales, thinking about the badminton net
that used to be strung across the grass next to the woods,
unable to move in any direction.

PLACES TO FEEL

The grocery store—if you go alone:
reach deep for frozen Brussel sprouts or peas,
close slowly the frosted glass door.
Your tears will stiffen on your skin,
easy to flick off before other shoppers notice.

Or—your womblike car, when the kids stay home,
surrounded by the music they mock, but
which reaches some part of you, mostly unreachable.

Not in the park: too many other mothers
or fathers who crowd the jungle gyms,
yelling direction to their aspiring Olympic offspring
to hide their own loneliness.

The safest place is the shower.
You can lock the door
with enough time so no other's needs interrupt,
and the water can stream across your skin
like kindness.

If not, someday your body will lock up,
shoulders and back in catatonic rigidity,
hives blossoming wetly beneath stressed skin,
old injuries protesting like tired children
moaning in the late afternoon.

Your best bet is to weep silently,
letting it leach from your bones
through muscle, down the nerve pathways
and out through that carapace you've built
into the light and electric air.

LIST OF LOST PHOTOGRAPHS

1. The Marais: Herve the Pigeon, looking for lunch, sipped at a puddle at our feet outside yet another church, while Americans in a tour group tipped their guide a meager euro or two, then slipped away to the Metro.
2. Burned Notre Dame and the cranes working on her, at night, lights spread along the crane's edge to warn air traffic, as if there were a ladder in the sky one could cross and reach the flying buttresses, climb down to explore the charred ruins.
3. Children in Sarlat's main square, running, running, age and time running after them.
4. In the CLUNY: the Lady and the Unicorn, a tapestry series apparently, they say, depicting the senses, but the Lady aged during the tapestries from young to old, and why does no one talk about that?
5. A middle-aged woman in gold ankle boots: Where is she going as she bicycles off across the cobblestone plaza on a Saturday night?
6. James "Joyce," the white husky on the square by the Sorbonne where we ate dinner the first night and we talked to Julie from Quebec sitting at the table next to us about dogs we've lost and how she fell this morning between the subway and the platform and was bruised all the way up to her hip. And could have died.
7. Simone de Beauvoir's grave, covered with lip-sticked kisses and thank yous. I am too grown up, too afraid of germs, even though I remember the moment I chose her book from the library shelf. How often must they clean her grave? Who will clean mine?

MACY

Then, last night a newish friendship—or a friendship renewed after a COVID hiatus—or a friendship that never got started because of COVID that we're now feeling our way toward—and we're drinking wine in a Ridgefield bar with all the doors open on a September afternoon, light like slowly snowing gold flakes floating down onto untrimmed grass, macadam and boxwood, and she tells me she's recently undergone a complete hysterectomy—at forty-five—her blonde and slender self, long fingers reaching for the stem of the wine glass as she states she's fine—*fine*—and she wishes people would stop asking with that overly caring tone of voice as if she was going to drop dead tomorrow and, sure, the doctors recommended taking both breasts as well, but then she went to MSK and they said they'd watch it closely— every four months into the city for tests—*but that's better, right?*—and the light sifts in and I wonder as I resist reaching to hug her—too soon, too intimate?—if some unconscious part of me secretly seeks out the dying.

THE SISTER OF MY OLDEST FRIEND DIES OF LUNG CANCER

I'm out walking and crying for my friend's loss and about
how hard it was for her to watch her sister slowly disappear,
and how the last time I saw my friend, when we had dinner
in New York with industrial chic tables and large glasses
of wine, she said, *we treat animals better than we treat the
dying,* and *all I think about is death: when I wake up, when
I fall asleep, when I'm working,* and I know what she means
and I cry for myself and for all the losses around me, and
the people driving by must wonder what's wrong with me,
if they look up from their own problems—and why should
they?—and I turn into Lakota Oaks, the conference center
that's going to be a school but used to be a monastery, and
you can see the monks' graveyard at the top of the hill
from the long beautiful pond around which I now walk the
remaining stations of the cross, an unbeliever amidst the
incomprehensible universe, and I think: *The universe is big
enough to hold my grief without getting hurt itself. I don't have
to carry it all,* and the man who was running the trail in the
opposite direction passes me again, saying, *beautiful day,* and
it almost is.

AND THEN FRANK

Staunch atheist, who made sacred music float from his piano keys and from our mouths loosened by his wines: now, around his thin bones his blood is daily washed, pressure spiking and diving, heart speeding up as if he were newly in love, fluid in his lungs, his breathing raspy and wet, in and out of the hospital from Thanksgiving to New Years, then just in. He decided he couldn't go on. How do we, without him?

AND ANOTHER

Grief makes me hollow, fragile
like glass blown too thin,
cooled too swiftly,
and all I want is to crouch,
rigid, holding my shape,
so nothing splinters—
but you—
you want to hold me,
comfort, but if you
touch me,
this cylinder that's
barely holding
the air inside it
will s h a t t e r

THIS IS WHAT GRIEF DOES

I cannot
                anymore
the ground is damp and moldy,
water cracking in icy layers over mud
crushed

What do I see?
I remember helpless laughter
            but now

where are you?

Granite rises up

We wait, shivering,
crackled into ice shavings

weeping soil covers you

The morning star is shrouded in fog,
and the new year stalks us,
relentless and half frozen.

PRAYER

The left eye, the stronger one, of course,
keeps developing itches, swellings,
red bubbles that scratch.
Occasional flashes of light—
that ophthalmologist's question
to which "yes" strikes fear.
But, the doctor assures me,
the tissue is healthy and
if I'm not getting floaters,
I can relax.

More than flashes of light,
what I long for is light itself:
glitter, flicker, slow burn
sunrise, voluptuous slow sunset,
cloudy, muted tones, crystal blues,
fading grey-yellow of a storm.

And when I look up from my work,
the sun seeps over the winter woods,
golden brown and grey,
gleaming bark, shadows hiding under
fallen leaves. Even barrenness
shows her beauty
when caressed by a beam.

God, keep me from living in darkness.

WHAT IT COMES DOWN TO

no matter how
many brownies I bake
or hugs I give or scented
candles or bottles of wine I gift,
no matter the hours grading papers
to help my student be stronger, smarter,
or hours of conversation with you, books
or poems written, numbers of squirrels
fed or butternut squash harvested,
bills paid, sinks scrubbed,
birthday cakes frosted,
it's not enough to
save you from
dying.

LOVE POEM

Darling, late afternoon has arrived.
Around us, lovers lose each other to twilight;
fearful winter is near. Sit with me.
Let us read poems together, our *Atlantis* as yet
undiscovered, still drowned.
Let us drink cabernet franc
and eat baguettes and brie before the fire
burns it all down. One moment.
It's what we have left.

SUMMER'S END

Some mornings helicopters thump
the blue apart, set dogs
whining and howling.
Airbrakes on the highway
rumble trees, airplanes
fizz across sky,
an occasional teen roars
his motorcycle up our hill.

This morning, though,
I woke to a deer and two fauns,
one curled on the grass, grazing
my weeds. Bees buzz thick
among mint and chive flowers.
It's quiet but for the oven's tick
as I dry tomatoes, listen to steady
acorn rain popping the deck: squirrels
preparing for winter.

GRATITUDE

This morning on my walk I saw a branch reaching into the road, its leaves pockmarked and shredded by traffic bustling by and I felt the need to touch it, as if to say, *someone sees your pain* and *someone knows you were here, trying to survive the drought, trying to clean the air, still trying to give us what we need, even as we abuse you* and once I see that gift, I see it everywhere: crabgrass lush on dry ground, the dandelion's sunny yellow smile, dogwoods struggling against wilt, cloud curled around a pop of blue sky. Who am I amidst this bounty but a thief, a pinprick in this wide, wide universe?

HOW TO GRIEVE

For months now grief has waited,
overflowing at maudlin TV
or the color of leaves
or my lover's inattention.

It has taken laming me,
my hip in constant aching pain,
to get me to feel the sticky, infected lake
of tears I'm carrying in my chest.

Grief is black, dangerous muck
that has clogged, thick and viscous,
around the drain, so that now
when the acupuncturist—
that kid with long curly hair
and enthusiasms,
his wide-eyed child
playing in a crib
in the waiting room—
presses on a spot on my foot,
the pain pooled there has so condensed
that, released, it makes me cry all afternoon.

And the only word that floats up
is *gratitude*,
that generosity toward the world
that opens me like surgery,
like sluice gates
that lower the level.

Laurel S. Peterson is a Professor of English at Connecticut State Community College. Her poetry has been published in many small literary journals. She has two poetry chapbooks, *That's the Way the Music Sounds* (Finishing Line Press) and *Talking to the Mirror* (Last Automat Press), and two full-length collections, *Do You Expect Your Art to Answer?* and *Daughter of Sky* (Futurecycle Press). She co-edited a collection of essays on women's justice titled *(Re)Interpretations: The Shapes of Justice in Women's Experience* (Cambridge Scholars Publishing) and has written two mystery novels *Shadow Notes* and *The Fallen* (Woodhall Press). She served on the editorial board of the literary magazine *Inkwell*, and as the town of Norwalk, Connecticut's, Poet Laureate from April 2016—April 2019. Currently, she sits on the Norwalk Public Library Board. You can find her on Substack at
https://laurelspeterson.substack.com/archive
and at her website: https://www.laurelpeterson.com/.